Delicate
A Collection of Poems by Chanel Hardy

Copyright© 2021 Chanel Hardy

All rights reserved. No part of this publication may be reproduced, distributed, or transmitted in any form or by any means, including photocopying, recording, or other electronic or mechanical methods, without the prior written permission of the publisher, except in the case of brief quotations embodied in critical reviews and certain other noncommercial uses permitted by copyright law. For permission requests, write to the publisher.

Printed in the United States of America

Hardy Publications

chardypublications.com

Angelica; Inspiration. The Black woman's pen is a mighty weapon. Our words, a battlefield. Fighting the wars of intersectional adversity for years on end.

Foreword by Jennifer P. Bush-Harris

Roxanne Gay said if Black writers are not encouraged and nurtured among other Black writers, who will? It is with this adage and wisdom that I am proud to know Chanel Hardy.

I met Chanel through the Facebook group Big Black Chapters in 2019. I found this Facebook group, founded by the writer duo of Tiffany Richardson and Raquel Shante de Lemos, through my bold adventuring through social media. It was a place of encouragement, humor, and education, with diligent determination for those of us being both Black and writer. For this boldness, I was rewarded with a family of writers who has determined to behave as Mother Morrison and Father Baldwin dictate: having language being the measure of our lives.

I thought my hustle was unique, with its own clip and pace, until I met like-minded writers determined to master both day and night--creating stories and paying bills in the same twenty-four hours. Chanel and I struck up an unlikely but expected friendship through posts about book reviews, making time to write, and the trash way in which Black writers are treated. In the two years I have known Chanel, I have seen her determination increase when it comes to mastering her talent! I have seen her grow into a maturing writer voice: becoming more vocal in her political views, teaching English abroad, and taking select English classes to strengthen her analysis.

In short, it has been a joy to watch Chanel occupy a broadening space as a writer with all her attributes. This is why I am glad I had the chance to interview her during the first season of my podcast platform, The Writers' Block. With that growth, Chanel has taken her fans and readers with her! From her more inclusive works *(Fernando, My Colorblind Rainbow),* poetry collections *(Sweet Oleander, I Had A Dream About You),* delving to the supernatural *(The Moonlight Series)* to her first epistolary novel *(P.S. I Hope This Finds You),* I can say this with complete confidence: Chanel is a writer's writer. She is diligent about her craft, committed to challenging it, all while harnessing it in order to create other opportunities. From these opportunities, she makes room for other writers to benefit from her knowledge while remaining the constant student.

When you encourage a writer, the world opens up. When that writer is Black, they can re-create it, bending it with their pens. Continue to bend the world, Chanel. Continue to bend the world.

Jennifer P. Bush-Harris
Founder, The Ideal Firestarter
Executive Producer, The Writers' Block
Freelance Author and Editor

Special thanks to those who enjoy my poems and listen to my podcast! Who watch my ramblings in real time on social media and encourage my writing journey, in all the ways it manifests.

-Chanel

Rue; Grace, clear vision. I see the past for what it was now. And my future for the seeds I have yet to sow.

Sometimes I look at the Sun

Sometimes I look at the Sun and wonder what it's like to watch us burn
she takes a seat on the edge of the sky and looks down at us

never asking why
or attempting to understand the plot at all
or question the storyline of this script called "mankind" a docudrama
of what it means to exist and be a being

sometimes I look at the sun in wonder
how bored she has to be to sit and struggle through this shit show
she must be lonely
all her children, the stars have left and started their own families

so she sits and spends eternity doing what any lonely mother would do
turn to Mindless entertainment to fill the void

sometimes I look at the Sun and pity her because I know what it feels like to live and she doesn't
to be more than a provider for others who never return the favor

I'm thankful that I'm not the Sun.

For Tracy

Tracy Chapman on repeat and a pen in my hand
this is what freedom feels like for me

her guitar strings tie me into this chair
and her fingers pull at the strings of my heart

telling stories of fast cars and talkin' bout a revolution
music truly is the gift that keeps on giving

I could write a thousand poems
and all I'd need is just one song one note to keep on living

All Those Women Back Then

Fifteen cents to her name
Three more quarters and a dime, and she might've
been able to buy herself some sense.

A minimum wage life with a minimally made man
The fifties, you see
Was a different time, entirely

Your aunties and mamma told you to find a mister
and keep your panties clean
Cook his dinner
Mind his manners and keep his drawers clean

And his work shirts
And his socks

And every little crease and corner between the fridge
and the sink

And when you see his eyes on the neighbor boy's
face
Just keep your head down and look the other way

All those women back then
And all those broken dreams

Next to the chest of drawers and underneath the
floorboards
She kept a box of all the things she'd do

if her life wasn't given away to some man in a tie and
a tan homburg hat

She kept photos of Paris that were cut out of
magazines
And dreams of a sunset behind the Eiffel tower

Photos that curl at the ends and smell of mothballs
and memories she never had.

And underneath her hopes and dreams in that box
Was fifteen cents.

Maybe if she had just a little bit more sovereignty
She might've been able to buy herself some time.

*W*oman/Bitch;(noun)

Being a woman is...
complex complicated convoluted

We are...
intricate exquisite
well-read and resilient

all things that can be synonyms for bitch
broad
shrew

but I beg you to call me by any other name
and i command you to respect my existence
my presence is a right not a privilege

you need us to birth you
not in a literal sense but figuratively speaking
the earth is a mind map and women are at the top
above your disdain and complete disregard for what it
means to be female

but I beg you
to call me by any other name
because a female is a synonym for bitch
but I prefer woman

Magnolia

A flower blooms that is you
Beneath the snow, underneath the soil of sorrow
I know, that *yo*u wait for me
and I wait for you

if only flowers bloom in the winter
then I could have something to hold onto
but all that comes when the snow falls is the memory
of the sun setting into your hair

I long of you
for spring
when the flower that is you blooms again

Like a whisper
you softly made your way into my heart
your tender voice telling me to come away with you
to watch the sunset

so I take you in hand, to the edge
and watch as the stars set into your hair

my eyes are wide in awe of the beauty that faces the
river before me
the day ends but the imprint of the grace it
leaves behind is everlasting

as everlasting as my love for you
for the beauty is not in the sun
but in you.

Magnolia; Love of nature. The grass only grows where the heart grows fonder.

They were all yellow
Melting like sweet lemon drops
Flaming in the sun.

Delicate: Poems by Chanel Hardy

Her alarm buzzes
The Statue of Liberty
Scowls at her children.

Boys in smug smiles
I never know what they want
They prey, and we pray.

Delicate: Poems by Chanel Hardy

The darkness looms here
Oh, I wonder what it wants
Quite possibly, me.

Dark Crimson Rose; Mourning. Each day passes and all that lasts is the memory. The melody of their face is a repetition that will never cease.

Ain't No Cliffhanger for This Ending

Rockets glare behind me
the 1% stuff prized possessions in their Prada bags
God's children beg for mercy forgiveness

embracing
their fate, but I'm not ready for mine
I still got stories to write, it ain't my time

but the bombs make their debut
and out from within, my spirit moves
As the world ends right before my eyes
I ask myself what's the point?
who am I writing for?

the world is too preoccupied with tending to its own demise to be bothered with me
The pages of my 5 by 8s cover the Moon
The world goes dark and it's just me alone

I ask God if I can bring my laptop into heaven and he says girl, read the room
and I laugh
and as the cloud of annihilation makes its way over to us
I sit poised and at peace and I tell myself

I regret nothing.

Making Love in Hardcovers

Lift Me Up
Above the Clouds
before I sleep Run your fingers through my pages
your soft skin melting between my sheets

This chapter of my life is one that I've never read before
the footnotes at the edge of this bed tell me that
you've been here before

references to Hughes, Brooks, Angelou and Wheatley
the prose from your mouth speaks foreign letters into
my skin

The endless possibilities of stories we can tell in the
sanctum of this bed never gets old
the tropes keep circulating between folds
just how I like it
Slow... prolonged with ease...

Please, before we close the shades and wrap up
This book of love
read your desires to me one more time
no bookmarks this time...
 just one more page.

We Are Earth

Don't you know that you're the ocean?
not AN ocean
THEE ocean
as in there's only one of you

other bodies of water can exist within our universe
but none cover the earth
and rise above the skyline of antiquated cities like
you do

The white gaze tells us a different story
that we are only Lakes
dried up revine's that serve no purpose

The white gaze means being forced to see the world
through a white person's eyes
but now times have changed
the only gaze I see is the one that shows me the
fluorescent waves of you
the black woman

an endless body of mystery
the sun reflects off you
and when days turn to night the moon rest his head
onto you

nestled between your bosom
and kept warm by the passion that burns within you
within us

*W*e are the ocean
the mountains

the sky
the stars
the moon
the sun

we are the mothers that give birth to the
sons of the earth
We are the earth.
We are God.

A Rolling Blackout

A rolling Blackout comes through and sweeps across the streets
turning bright brown faces into Shadow Shades of Grey

a rolling blackout traps The Souls of the Dead in AC filters
sweats clogs the pores of the poor
while they scramble to find the space to breathe

In a rolling blackout
chaos lurks under the hoods of street boys
tucked inside the waist belts of the desperate

have you ever tried to sleep during a blackout?
even your dreams can't escape the shadows
or the heat no one knows how long it will be
before the power comes back

but the thing about a blackout is
the ones who suffer the most
never had any power to begin with

U Matter

Run to me
I am here
Run to me before the wrath of obscurity swallows you whole and no one remembers.

No one remembers what you said
Or how you made them feel
but I'm here
I feel you

I can feel you drifting away
I can hear the interlude into your songs
The prologue into your despair

Your life's greatest work will go down in history
But there is no history without you to make it so
So... Hold on for just a little bit longer

The world needs your artistry
your vision,
your lust for life to make it stronger.

I don't know who told you that you didn't matter
But they were wrong
You do matter

Your essence keeps hope alive
You do matter
Your art keeps the girl from diving into catatonia
when she believes nothing else matters.

So run to me

Let me save you from yourself
The world needs you now more than ever.

An Al Green Erasure Poem

I'm so tired ▇▇▇▇▇▇▇▇▇▇▇▇▇▇▇▇▇▇▇▇
▇▇▇▇▇▇▇▇▇▇▇▇▇▇▇▇▇▇▇▇
▇▇▇▇▇▇▇ I've found a way ▇▇▇▇▇▇▇▇▇▇▇
▇▇▇▇▇▇▇ I wanna come back ▇▇▇▇▇▇▇▇
▇▇▇▇▇▇▇▇▇▇▇▇▇▇▇▇▇▇▇▇
Won't you help me ▇▇▇▇▇▇▇▇▇▇▇▇
▇▇▇▇▇▇▇▇▇▇▇▇▇
▇▇▇▇▇▇▇ don't want me ▇▇▇▇▇
▇▇▇▇▇▇▇▇▇▇▇▇▇▇▇▇▇▇▇▇
▇▇▇▇▇▇▇▇▇▇▇▇▇▇▇▇▇▇▇▇
▇▇▇▇▇▇▇▇▇▇▇▇▇▇▇▇▇▇▇▇
▇▇▇▇▇▇▇▇▇▇▇▇ being all wrapped up ▇▇▇▇
In my dreams, ▇▇▇▇▇▇▇▇▇▇▇▇ I wonder
▇▇▇▇▇▇▇▇▇▇▇▇
You see ▇▇▇▇ I been thinkin' about it, ▇▇▇▇▇
▇▇▇▇▇▇▇▇▇▇▇▇▇▇▇▇▇▇▇▇
You ▇▇▇▇▇▇▇▇▇▇▇▇▇▇▇▇▇▇
▇▇▇▇▇▇▇▇▇▇
▇▇▇▇▇▇▇▇▇▇▇▇▇▇▇ my greatest dream, ▇▇▇
▇▇▇▇▇▇▇ of being alone ▇▇▇▇▇

Lily; Beauty. The blueprint. No man has the courage to ask her name. Even God himself fumbles at the sight of her.

I love how love tastes
Sometimes it lingers, bitter
Then it goes down strong.

Delicate: Poems by Chanel Hardy

The beauty in me
Only shines if you touch it
Burns out when you don't.

The tapestry here
Was crafted with grace
The finest of silk

Delicate: Poems by Chanel Hardy

Being a woman, now
When patience is a virtue
Feels like punishment.

Midnight pulls up late
I grab my shoes to go with
Then he leaves me cold.

Delicate: Poems by Chanel Hardy

Red Columbine; Anxious, trembling. How I forget to breathe when his hand brushes the nape of my neck.

Delicate

He runs his hands across my knees and wonders why they're so dark.

I tell him about the long nights I spent on the floor in the trenches.

He runs his hands along the lines of the wrinkles in my face
and asks why I look so aged

I tell him about the memories of war and all the battles I fought to survive.

He holds my shoulders and compliments how broad they are.

I tell him it's from years of having to stand firm on my own.

I am strong.

But when he brushes my hair back and kisses the nape of my neck
I'm reminded that I am delicate too.

Body

My hair ain't straight and my hips ain't small
but my mouth is loud like a firecracker
my bones pop when I move too fast
but so do my lips

my body is heavy but my heart is always light
there will always be space in me to love
to give and to receive

so don't count me out because my hair ain't straight
and my hips ain't small
and my skin ain't light

there is more to take from me than what you see.

Complicit

Why do our tongues fill the back of our throats when
we attempt to scream?
Silence is complicit.

There is no pain when there is no voice.
"Just let me kill you and I'll tell them you enjoyed it.
Speak now or forever hold your pain."

But I am not complicit
and neither are you

so they will not take our lives away from us and tell
the story of when they hurt us and we allowed it
We did no such thing

The voice once held down by the tight grips of their
hands
is now free to tell the truth and set us free use these
lines as a balance beam to reach the other side to
freedom

and when I get across
when we get across
crowds will gather in our honor to hear us speak
and kill the narrative that silence equals rapture.

Moonlight with You

When the moon howls
will you stay and catch it with me?

When the sky turns who will watch it with me when
you're gone?

I don't want the night if I can't have you with it.
I don't want the daylight to come and the sun to touch
my skin if you can't touch it too.

I'd rather live in a world of frenzy instead of a world
of blue torn moons.

My Hair in Rainbow Colors

Semi-permanent dye mixes like the color palettes of famous films

Full length films that are earth tone shades of Blue is the Warmest Color
like my hair

and when The Revenant ends I strip what's left and add a touch of Moonlight
neon violet

that pops and fades when the credits roll and when the seasons change I look for warmth

so I dive into the depths of the Atlantic in hopes that the Titanic still has some sandstone and Marigold at the bottom of the bottle for me

and if not then I'll just have to make my own.

Zinnia; Thoughts of absent friends.
Permanent beings and passing fancies.
Those who come and go, and those
who never stay.

Call out to God
The line hasn't been severed yet
You've got one dime left

Delicate: Poems by Chanel Hardy

My coffee is cold
Its bitter taste more raised now
My morning woes, await.

My nails are brittle
Vitamin deficiency
Skin, pales in comparison.

Time passes, waves rush
The sea calls for me to run
Swim, into its arms.

Violet; Loyalty, devotion, faithfulness, modesty. All qualities women must keep tucked in the pockets of our dresses. But when have dresses ever been designed with pockets in mind?

Enclosed

I play a game of i-spy to pass the time

I spy with my little eye
satin fabric, ruffled at the edges puncture-resistant, leak-proof
but the bugs find their way in anyway

dirt
mold
the egg sacs of a spider who has found her forever home, in my forever home

I spy with my little eye
darkness
darkness
darkness

I don't even know how long it's been since my funeral

but I play i-spy to pass the time.

THIRTY

To all the days I've loved before. A love letter to my ex-years.

How have you been? Lets not be strangers anymore. I know you better than you know myself.

I know time doesn't change things, but you owe it to me to give yourself another chance. That's what you do for people you love.

Rhythm of sound flows through my ears, and I can hear my old self singing 'Glory Days.' Where did the good times go?

To all the seconds that grew into minutes, that grew into hours too ashamed to let father time kiss it's cheek goodbye.

Years really do run together like acrylic colors that blend to form the art that is womanhood.

And **Thirty** is the fresh canvas you get to paint it on.

The Hills

Put our colors together and tell me what you get
nothing pales in comparison to the salmon shades of
pink the universe gets to see when you smile

blend these blues with crimson red and watch the
hues of violet hills wash over the fields of buttercups

that stretch far beyond anything we could ever create
together

I'm not familiar with this palette but I'm no stranger to
trying new things

there was a point in time when you were unfamiliar
too

but we put our colors together and what we made was
beautiful

so let's do it again.

Delicate: Poems by Chanel Hardy

A Nora Jones Erasure Poem

~~━━━━━━━━━~~
~~━━━━━━━━━~~
~~━━━━━━━━━~~
~~━━━━━━━━━~~
~~━━━━━~~ *tempt us,* ~~━━━━~~
~~━━━━━~~
On a cloudy day
~~━━━━━━━━━~~
~~━━━━━━━━━~~
~~━━━━━━━~~ *we'll kiss*
~~━━━━━~~
~~━━━━━~~
And I'll never stop loving you
~~━━━━━━━~~
Falling ~~━━━━━~~
~~━━━━━~~ *in your arms*
~~━━━━━~~
~~━━━━━~~ *in the night*
~~━━━━━~~

Justacia Carnea

Some say the Brazilian plume flower is the blood of Jesus
it heals and protects the heart

some say that the Brazilian plume flower is a hospital too far

it's rich color nourishes the sick

its foliage crushed and blended to save us all
like Jesus himself

Justacia Carnea, mother nature's Lord and savior.

Grown

My favorite thing about being an adult is that I can have chocolate chip cookies and cheesecake for dinner

I can raise my own blood pressure for breakfast and have sharp leg pains is a midday snack

my favorite thing about being an adult is having sex and not having to lie to my parents about it

having sex and getting a urinary tract infection because I forgot to pee afterwards

having sex and not caring about my 10th pregnancy scare

my least favorite thing about being an adult is having full autonomy over a body that feels me daily

Sweet Pea; Delicate pleasures. The first bite into a freshly opened chocolate bar. The way his bittersweet kisses melt on my tongue.

Diabetic love
My body can't take your taste
It's killer contents.

Delicate: Poems by Chanel Hardy

Passion is fleeting
Bring it here, so we can stay
I don't want it to leave us.

I'm not sure you know
The thought is imperative
Only secrets die.

Darkness lives in her
The light creeps out when she cums
Then retreats half mast.

Begonia; Dark thoughts. Women are versatile lovers. The knife that slits his throat also cuts his pancakes. Women are versatile lovers. The knife that slits his throat also cuts his pancakes.

Starlight Express

I navigate using star light to find my way through
your madness
red eyes running hot brown eyes holding tight dark
circles under my eyelids

how can I sleep when you're running hot moving fast
like a fever dream on acid
the light doesn't flicker not even once
but it's dark outside now and we need the light to
guide us

there is a hole at the edge of the window
it's small but maybe if we stretch it wide enough
just enough so one of us can make our way through it

if you let me go I promise I'll come back for you
I promise
have I ever broken a promise to you?

the darkness won't last long and we'll be together
again
cruising down the highway with our dreams on max
volume madness riding through our starlight express

"Show me where it's at, Baby"

When I was a kid my mother would listen to Al Green pretty much all the time. So much that his lyrics was sewn into my skin with the nude kind of thread that nobody can see.

Not even me.

I forgot they were there until a few weeks ago when tired of being alone came on through my bluetooth headphones and I remembered every sound

every word
every melody
every chord

every single reason why my mother played his music so much. Then I played all his records.
every verse
every bridge
every chorus

every single lyric that made me wonder what it was like to own an entire decade of longing souls.

Recipe for Disaster

Ingredients
2 oz of chestnut brown
1 lb of Yaki 1B
160 lb of melanin (raw not the cheap store brand kind)
1 stick of pink matte lipstick
1 roll-on clear gloss to cover her lips
2 door knocker bamboo earrings (silver not gold) one spoonful of her mom's attitude one ceramic bowl

Directions
Step 1 pour all ingredients into a bowl and mix well.
Step 2 mix until it creates a dark thick like substance.
Step 3 pour into an 8 x11 round pan.
Step 4 don't forget to preheat the oven to 350 but it's probably too late now. You'll have to set it a few degrees higher and monitor her progress
Step 5 if she's not perfect it'll be a recipe for disaster.
Step 6 if she's not well spoken or proper she'll never get a job, fit in, be a respectable black to make her parents proud.
Step 7 don't let her burn she's a delicate treat
Step 8 remove from the oven let sit for 10 minutes.

Enjoy.

A Dream Job Sounds Like a Nightmare

When people ask me what my dream job is I tell them nothing
I do not dream of the labor
I do not dream of working

My true dream
my true passion
is to drink iced coffee as I sit and stare at the wall
Simply just existing

No deadlines no quotas.
No timesheets no anal bosses.
No outlines no pantsing.
Nothing

My dream job is to be an entrepreneur of no jobs.
A legal assassin of "what do you do for a living?"
Cutting the throats of that dreaded question yuppies like to ask
so they can know how much respect you deserve to be paid

The next time someone asks, "If you could work your dream job, what would you be doing?"
I'm going to say "Not standing here and talking to you. Don't you have anything else better to do? Go stare at a wall or something."

When people ask me what my dream job is, I tell them the truth.
I dream of nothing
a dream job sounds like a nightmare.

Father!

Come, girl, tell me your sin.

Father God, for I have sinned, forgive me.
I have stolen the cup that runeth over and hoarded my riches from the world.

Fear not, you are forgiven.
Or not
No, your sins don't matter.

Why not? Why now?
Father, redemption is all I have.
What good is sin, if not to be forgiven?
Cast me out and bring me back.
Wipe me clean and prepare my bed in heaven.

Get off your knees girl and stop this madness!
What does my approval matter if it is not needed?
Fear not the depths of hell, or heaven.

Father!

Fear not.

My lord and savior!
In heaven
My lord, my savior
My god
My sins
My guilt
My savior
Please, forgive me.

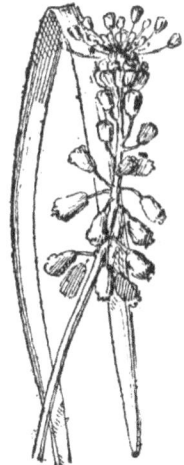

Yellow Hyacinth; Jealousy. Her rage grows green with envy. Rotting to the core. Little does she know, the other woman is rotting too.

Body lies daily
Tells me what to want and crave
Then bans me from it.

Flowers are like maps
They guide to new beginnings.
And end where peace goes.

I'm guilty of sin
But I love it, what I do
Transgression, my flair.

Delicate: Poems by Chanel Hardy

Black is a virtue
But treated as a misdeed
Only whiteness can thrive here.

Tell me what you want
I can pull tricks out of ice
And pull love out of thin air.

Amaryllis; Pride. I can think of a million ways to apologize, and a million more reasons why I won't.

Plush

You hold me when nobody else does
you keep me warm when the cold chill creeps from
behind the walls

You're the perfect hiding spot away from my
problems
I still remember the day I bought you home for the
first time.

I undressed and let you wrap yourself around me
we got in bed and I kept you pressed against me

it hasn't been a year yet
but I know I want you in my life forever
I know I'll need you as a means of comfort

so I hope you stay
I'd hate to buy another blanket.

Delicate & Black

When they know you're delicate
all they want to do is touch
rub their hands in places they don't belong and pull
away

when you're too rough, they recoil
not good enough
they say we're not good enough
to love and to hold

no vulnerability to pick at so they fly away
back to their nest of wives and hungry children
and you go back to your shell
what's left of it

when they know you're delicate
they crack the shell too

now you're nothing
but they prefer us that way.

Get Free

One of these days, Black women gotta get free
simping for patriarchy is not the move, sis
he still wont pick you
hasn't picked you yet
no matter how many times you tell him McDonald's
is a date
or you'll make his plate
first
and let the kids burn in a house fire
there is no gold medal for the pick-me Olympics
but you might get a participation trophy
maybe he'll throw you some scraps if you're lucky.

This Is an Invitation

Imagine a world where Valentine's Day is everyday

now imagine a world where every day is your mortal enemy's birthday

they throw an extravagant party where everyone in the world is invited but you
every day

You watch the fun from your window and smell the cake from the kitchen
Carrot with cream cheese icing, your favorite
that bitch
every day

it's the same thing

Someone once asked me what being in my head was like
and this was my answer.

Blue Eyes

Blue eyes are the reason why the comb pulls at my scalp
why my momma tells me to stop crying before she gives me something to cry about

blue eyes are the reason why the popular girl pulled my scarf off in gym class sin the 7th grade and laughed
everyone laughed

bue eyes are the reason why I cut the hair off my black barbie doll to make them Kens when my white barbies didn't get a boyfriend for Christmas

blue eyes are the reason why I never got a boyfriend for Christmas

blue eyes are the reason why I wrote Emily's name in the back of my borrowed library book in 1st grade instead of my own name because I wanted to be her

Emily didn't have blue eyes, but someone along the lines of her biracial gene pool did
those blue eyes, the ones our ancestors stared into all those centuries ago

when the Europeans first cracked the whip and told them that his blue eyes would haunt their children and grandchildren and set the rules for their daughters and granddaughters self-esteem

blue eyes are the reason why I wrote this poem
why I write at all
why it's important for Black women and girls to know that even without blue eyes, we are the blueprint

the beauty that reigns supreme
we are delicate.

White Chrysanthemum; Truth. I tell no lies here, but your perception is not my responsibility. Take what you see with a grain of salt. But beware, sugar rears its ugly head too.

Thanks for Reading! Don't forget to rate and review on amazon or Goodreads!

Check out other titles by me!

I Had A Dream About You: A Collection of Poems

Sweet Oleander: A Collection of Poetry

Fernando

My Colorblind Rainbow

River's Moonlight

The Coldest Moon

The Harvest Moon: A Prequel

Was It Her?

Mahogany Tales

Also Follow me on social media

@chanelhardypub_

Delicate: Poems by Chanel Hardy

ABOUT THE AUTHOR

Born and raised in the Washington D.C. area, writing has been a passion of mine since I was young. I started writing my first book, 'My Colorblind Rainbow' in 2013. In 2017, I decided to continue writing, taking a leap of faith and following my dreams of publishing my first book which made the 'In the Margins Award Long List' for YA fiction 2018. I launched **Hardy Publications** in September of 2017, working as a freelance ghostwriter, author, and literary blogger. I also use my platform to raise awareness for different charities and non-profit organizations, donating a portion of my book royalties to help others in need.

Check out Hardy Publications Apparel & Accessories on Teespring.com!

www.ingramcontent.com/pod-product-compliance
Lightning Source LLC
Chambersburg PA
CBHW031457040426
42444CB00007B/1134